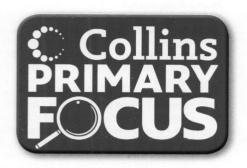

Comprehension
Pupil Book 4

John Jackman

William Collins' dream of knowledge for all began with the publication of his first book in 1819. A self-educated mill worker, he not only enriched millions of lives, but also founded a flourishing publishing house. Today, staying true to this spirit, Collins books are packed with inspiration, innovation and practical expertise. They place you at the centre of a world of possibility and give you exactly what you need to explore it.

Collins. Freedom to teach.

Published by Collins
An imprint of HarperCollins*Publishers* Ltd.
77–85 Fulham Palace Road
Hammersmith
London
W6 8JB

**Browse the complete Collins catalogue at
www.collinseducation.com**

Text © John Jackman 2011
Design and illustrations © HarperCollins*Publishers* 2011

Previously published as *Collins Primary Comprehension*, first published 1998; and *Collins Focus on Comprehension*, first published 2002.

10 9 8 7 6

ISBN: 978-0-00-741064-4

John Jackman asserts his moral right to be identified as the author of this work.

British Library Cataloguing in Publication Data
A Catalogue record for this publication is available from the British Library.

Cover template: Laing & Carroll
Cover illustration: Steve Evans
Series design: Neil Adams and Garry Lambert
Picture research: Gill Metcalfe
Illustrations: Meena Arnold, Maggie Brand, Rob Englebright, Rob Englebright, Robin Lawrie, Bethan Matthews, Andrew Midgley, Jakki Wood, Peter Bull, Shirley Chiang, Bridget Dowty, Kevin Hopgood, Gwyneth Williamson, Rosemary Woods

Acknowledgements
The author and publisher wish to thank the following for permission to use copyright material:
David Higham Associates Ltd for an extract from *Trouble Half-Way* by Jan Mark, Penguin Books, 1985. Reproduced by permission of David Higham Associates Ltd; Mrs A. W. Morse for an extract from "Crack-a-dawn" by Brian Morse, published in *Picnic on the Moon*, Turton and Chambers Ltd, 1990. Granted by kind permission of Mrs A.W. Morse; Curtis Brown Group, Inc for the poem "Winter Morning" by Ogden Nash from *Parents Keep Out 2nd edition*, Little Brown and Co, 1951, copyright © 1962 by Ogden Nash. Reprinted by permission of Curtis Brown Group, Ltd; Aitken Alexander Associates Ltd for an extract from *Wild Swans* by Jung Chang, first published by Simon & Schuster, copyright © Jung Chang, reproduced with permission from Aitken Alexander Associates Ltd; David Higham Associates Ltd and Farrar, Straus and Giroux, LLC for an extract from "Dream-Catching" from *The BFG* by Roald Dahl, Jonathan Cape & Penguin Books, 1982. Copyright © 1982 by Roald Dahl. Reproduced by permission of David Higham Associates Ltd and Farrar, Straus and Giroux, LLC; HarperCollins Publishers Ltd and Random House, Inc. for an extract from *The Phantom Tollbooth* by Norton Juster, copyright © 1962 and renewed 1989 Norton Juster, reproduced by permission of HarperCollins Publishers Ltd and Random House Children's Books, a division of Random House, Inc.; Penguin Group (USA) Inc. for an extract from *The TV Kid* by Betsy Byars, copyright © 1976 by Betsy Byars. Used by permission of Viking Penguin, a division of Penguin Young Readers Group, a member of Penguin Group (USA) Inc., 345 Hudson Street, New York, NY 10014. All rights reserved; and A P Watt Ltd for an extract from *Martin's Mice* by Dick King-Smith, reproduced by permission of A P Watt Ltd on behalf of Dick King-Smith.

Artwork pp54–56 © Rosemary Woods

Every effort has been made to trace copyright holders and to obtain their permission for the use of copyright material. The author and publishers will gladly receive any information enabling them to rectify any error or omission in subsequent editions.

Photographs
p19 top: Getty Images; p19 bottom: INTERFOTO/Alamy; p20: Getty Images; p22 top: Getty Images; p22 bottom: Rick Giase/epa/Corbis; pp35-36: Paul Souders/Corbis; p37: Dale O'Dell/Alamy; pp44-45: Stockbrokerxtra Images/Photolibrary; p62 Christophe Boisvieux/Corbis

Printed in Italy by L.E.G.O. S.p.A.

Contents

Trouble Half-Way

Amy's father has died and her mother's new husband has moved in.

For a start, Amy never knew what to call him. She would not, like Helen, call him Daddy and she knew he did not expect her to, but Step-Daddy sounded daft, and she could hardly call him Mr Ermins. Mum did not like her calling him Richard.

'You never called your Dad Michael, did you?' Mum had said unreasonably.

Usually she just made a mumbling noise. It was easier for him: she was Amy to everyone. No one would ever have called her daughter – not Dad, not Richard.

Mum was folding the napkins into even smaller squares ready for ironing.

'What d'you want to iron nappies for?' Richard would ask, sometimes. 'Helen won't know any different.'

'Oh, I don't know – it looks… nicer,' Mum would say.

'But no one can see them.'

'I can see them,' Mum would retort, looking at the tottering pile of flattened napkins on the table, like a stack of sandwiches waiting to be cut into quarters. Richard would be looking at the laundry basket on the floor, full of things still waiting to be ironed.

'Life's too short,' he would say.

Now he was looking at the elastic bandage around Amy's knee.

'How's your leg?'

Mum was looking at her socks but not saying anything. The socks were gyving round her ankles because she kept tugging at them during lessons and the stretchy part was giving way. Mum ironed socks, too.

'It's not too bad,' Amy said, meaning her knee, and added carefully, because it was Richard who had asked, 'thank you.'

'What do you mean, not too bad?' Mum said, quickly. 'Has it been hurting?'

'It twinged a bit this morning when I knelt down in assembly.'

'You be careful – you want it right for Thursday. Perhaps I ought to write a note and ask Miss Oxley to let you off games and that for the start of next week.'

'But I've got to practise,' Amy said. 'Anyway, Miss Oxley won't let me do anything I shouldn't. She says I'm the best chance we've got if Debra isn't better.'

'What's wrong with Debra?'

'She turned her ankle on the beam on Wednesday. She came down too heavy.' Amy noticed that Richard was staring at her over the rim of his mug.

'*Kneeling?*' he said. 'In assembly?'

'Yes.'

'Hands – together – eyes – closed – Our – Father – which – art – in – heaven?'

'Yes.'

'Good God,' said Richard.

'What did *you* do in assembly, then?' Mum demanded, unfolding the ironing board. 'Stand on one leg?'

Jan Mark

Do you remember?

Copy these sentences. Fill each gap.

1. Amy's mother's new husband is called _____ .
2. Amy's mum was getting ready to do the _____ .
3. _____ is Amy's teacher.
4. Debra hurt her _____ on the beam.
5. Mum asked Richard if he stood on one leg in _____ .

More to think about

1. Write a sentence to answer each question.
   a) What relation was Helen to Amy?
   b) Why did Amy need to get used to Mr Ermins?
   c) Why didn't her mother want Amy to call Mr Ermins Richard?
   d) Why did Richard think it was unnecessary to iron nappies?
   e) Why didn't Amy want to make a fuss about her bad knee?

2. What clues are there in the passage that show Amy's mum and Richard were feeling rather irritated with each other?

3. Find these phrases in the passage. Write them in your own words without changing the meaning.
   a) Mum would retort
   b) the tottering pile
   c) Life's too short
   d) The socks were gyving round her ankles

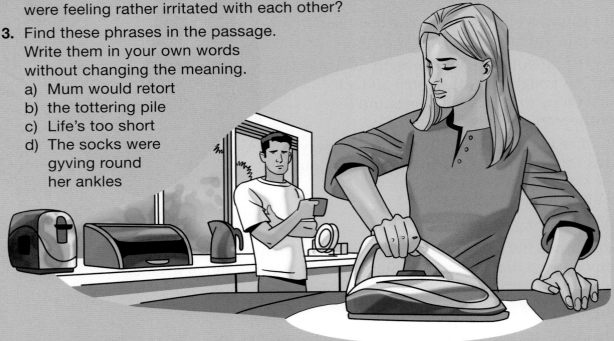

Now try these

1. Imagine that you are Amy. Write a letter to a friend describing Richard, your feelings about him and how you get on with him.

2. What do you think Amy should have called Richard? Give your reasons.

3. It is terribly sad if a parent dies, as Amy's father did. It can also be difficult for everyone when a mother or father brings a new partner to live with the family. What problems can you imagine for the children and for the new partner when this happens? Make two lists, using these headings:

Problems for the children	Problems for the new partner

Crack-a-Dawn

Good day and good morning!
Here is your early morning tea
and here are your crack-a-dawn cereals.
Sugar is also provided.
Breakfast in bed, room service calling!
Are you awake?

Darren, sit up I'm giving you
ten seconds, starting now! TEN.
The weather outside is fine – at least
by North Sea standards. NINE.
Just a fresh Force Six blowing and a spot
of rain lashing the rooftops. EIGHT.
The sun is shining – lucky Australians!
The bus, however, is on time
according to local radio – SEVEN –
and if you want to walk again and be
reported to the Head that is your business
but – SIX – I have a bus to catch too
and you can pay for a taxi out of your pocket money
if I miss it the third morning running.

FIVE. Your gerbil has been eaten by the dog
and the dog has been eaten by a crocodile
that got in down the chimney and is, at the moment,
opening its jaws over your toes –
feel it? No? Oh well.
FOUR. A letter has just arrived,
postmarked Wembley, inviting you to play
for England next Saturday against Czechoslovakia –
bet you won't be late for that. THREE.
Czechoslovakia was one of the eighteen spellings
wrong in your Geography homework.
Why wasn't it handed in last week? I found
the letter you forged from your dad
stating you had a dental appointment
on Friday afternoon – TWO – you could
at least have spelt his Christian name right
and the address. Make an appointment with him
an hour after you intend to go out tonight.

ONE. This is your mother speaking
and I am about to pour your tea
over your head, even if it causes me
extra washing. I won't begrudge the powder.
Darren, I'm giving you HALF A SECOND,
A QUARTER, AN EIGHTH.
No this is not a nightmare,
no the trickle of water you feel at this moment,
is NOT an illusion …

Brian Morse

Do you remember?

Write the correct answer to each question.

1. What was the boy's name?
   a) The boy's name was Darrel.
   b) The boy's name was Darren.

2. What did his mother give him for breakfast?
   a) His mother took him crack-a-dawn cereal for breakfast.
   b) His mother took him bacon and eggs for breakfast.

3. Where did she take Darren's breakfast?
   a) She took it to him in bed.
   b) She took it to him in his tent.

4. What was the weather like?
   a) The weather outside was windy and rainy.
   b) The weather outside was fine.

5. If he misses the bus, how is Darren to get to school?
   a) Darren will need to walk to school.
   b) Darren will need to go to school by taxi.

6. Whose name did Darren misspell?
   a) Darren misspelt his dad's name.
   b) Darren misspelt his mum's name.

7. Why was his mother cross?
   a) She was cross because she had missed her bus on the last two mornings.
   b) She was cross because she had missed her bus on the last three mornings.

More to think about

1. Write a sentence to answer each question.
   a) Why do you think the poem is called Crack-a-Dawn?
   b) What does Darren's mother mean by "the weather outside is fine – at least by North Sea standards"?
   c) Has the gerbil really been eaten by the dog? Why does Mum say it has?
   d) What is Darren's favourite sport?

2. Write a description of Darren's mum. Think carefully about the words you might use to describe her from the clues in the poem.

3. Write a brief summary of what happens in the poem, using no more than 30 words.

Now try these

1. What do you think happened in the end? Write four more lines for the poem.

2. Think of something else that you might count down to. Write a poem counting down from ten to zero and describing your feelings as the event draws closer. Your poem might look like this:

   TEN: _____
   NINE: _____
   EIGHT: _____

3. Write a nonsense verse. You could start your poem like this:

   If I were to lay all day in bed
   My dad would pour water on my head!
   If I were to …

4. We all have some habits that other people find annoying or irritating. Write about some of the things you do that make your friends or family cross.

The Trojan War

THE CAUSE OF THE TROJAN WAR

Troy was among the greatest cities in the ancient world. It was surrounded by mighty walls, so huge they were considered impenetrable. One of the Trojan princes who lived in the city was called Paris.

One day Paris travelled to Greece to meet the king, Menelaus, and Helen, his wife, who was undoubtedly the most beautiful woman he had ever set eyes on. Instantly Paris fell deeply in love with her; so deeply that he secretly asked her to go back to Troy and live with him there, for ever. Initially Helen would not hear of it, but eventually Paris persuaded her, and they secretly eloped while Menelaus was away from the country.

It is not difficult to imagine the king's bewilderment and anger when he returned. He sent his messenger to ask the Trojans to ensure the immediate return of Helen to Greece, but when the Trojans refused he brought together his best ships and bravest soldiers under the command of Agamemnon, his brother. It was thus that the Trojan War started.

THE GREEK HERO ACHILLES

Legend has it that one of the great Greek heroes who fought in the Trojan War was Achilles, a half-god, being the son of Zeus, the Greeks' most important god.

When he was a baby, Achilles' mother had dipped him in the magic waters of the Styx River. This meant every part of his body was thus protected from harm, except the heel by which his mother had held him when she dangled him in the waters. To give him extra power and strength his mother fed him on lion meat and the marrow from bears' bones. So it was that Achilles grew to become a strong, powerful soldier who could fight any battle, and without fear of ever being wounded!

One such battle led to the death of Paris's younger brother, Hector, but eventually Paris brought his revenge. One day, when Achilles was kneeling at prayer in the Temple of Apollo, Paris crept in and shot a poisoned arrow into his heel, killing the hitherto invincible hero. To this day, people talk of someone's Achilles' heel, meaning his or her weak point.

THE TROJAN HORSE

The brave warriors on both sides continued to fight and to die. Neither side seemed to be getting the upper hand in the conflict. In desperation, the Greek hero Odysseus devised a plan. They would build a huge wooden statue of a horse and leave it as a religious offering. Out of sight of the Trojans, they constructed the huge wooden horse, but unbeknown to the Trojans a large number of Greek warriors hid inside the hollow statue. Then the Greeks made a great issue about gathering together all their troops, boarding the ships and sailing away from Troy.

Delighted with the apparent retreat of their enemy, the Trojans opened the gates and flocked out of their city. As they were celebrating they came across the horse. Intrigued, they poked it and tapped it, and then found Sinon, a Greek soldier hiding nearby. They threatened him with swords and spears, forcing him, so they thought, to divulge the secret of the horse. Sinon said that if the Trojans 'captured' the horse, the Greeks would be so demoralised they would never return to threaten Troy again.

The Trojans were delighted! Their strongest man heaved and dragged the wooden monster into the city, needing to destroy part of the city wall in the process as it wouldn't fit through even the widest gate. That night there was a great celebration in Troy with feasts and dancing, and lots of liquor! Later, with everyone exhausted and sleeping soundly, Sinon crept up to the huge horse and released the Greek soldiers. Then he ran to open all the city gates to let in the other Greek soldiers, whose boats had returned under the cover of dark.

It was a rout! The Greeks totally destroyed the Trojan army before it could properly gather itself, and set fire to the city. Helen was taken captive and forced to return to King Menelaus, and the long, bloody, Trojan War ended.

Do you remember?

Read these sentences about the Trojan War.
Write 'true', 'false' or 'can't tell' for each one.

1. The Trojan War was fought between the people of Troy and Greece.
2. Most of the Greek soldiers came from the city of Athens.
3. Menelaus was the king of Greece.
4. His wife was Helen.
5. Paris forced Helen to run away with him.
6. They eloped while Menelaus was visiting his mother.
7. Achilles was the greatest hero Greece has ever had.
8. It was totally impossible for him to be killed.
9. The Greeks built the Trojan Horse.
10. The Greeks won the Trojan War, and Helen returned to Greece.

More to think about

1. In your own words, describe what caused the Greeks to declare war on the Trojans.
2. Why do you think Helen didn't go away with Paris as soon as he asked her?
3. What clues can you find in the passage to show that the two armies were fairly evenly matched?
4. Use a dictionary to help you match each of these definitions to a word in the grid. The first one has been done to help you.

	A	B	C
1	eventually	heaved	divulge
2	ensure	initially	intrigued
3	devised	instantly	invincible

   a) reveal, or let out   CI
   b) at once, or immediately
   c) in the end
   d) invent, or worked out
   e) lift with effort
   f) impossible to beat
   g) fascinated
   h) at first
   i) make sure
5. What do the following phrases mean? Write them in your own words.
   a) they secretly eloped
   b) the king's bewilderment and anger
   c) hitherto invincible hero
   d) unbeknown to the Trojans
   e) It was a rout!

Now try these

1. The Trojan War occurred thousands of years ago. Which parts of the passage do you think are true, and which parts might have become altered over the years?
2. Imagine that you are Odysseus. Write a letter to King Menelaus describing in detail your plan for winning the war, and explaining why you're sure it will work.
3. Can you think of a way that the Trojan War could have been resolved peacefully? Write a suggestion to one of the people mentioned in the passage.

The Discontented Fish

Once upon a time, in a small pool isolated from the main river, lived a colony of little fish. It was a still, muddy pool, stony and weedy, and surrounded by scraggy trees and bushes.

It was, nevertheless, a happy pool. Most of the fish were friendly and content. But there was one fish, bigger and stronger than all the others, who kept himself to himself. He was aloof and haughty whenever the others came near him.

'My good fellows,' he would say, balancing himself with his long, graceful tail as he rippled his fins gently, 'can't you see I'm trying to rest? Do please stop the commotion and respect my peace.'

'I wonder how you manage to put up with us at all,' said one of the older fish, who was becoming irritated by the big fish's constant gripes. 'I wonder why a beautiful creature like you doesn't go off to the big river and mix with the other big and important fish,' he added sarcastically.

This prompted the big fish to think further on how much too big and important he was to be living in such a small pool, and after a few days he decided to leave.

'My friend is quite right,' he thought. 'I should be far happier if I lived among fish of my own size, beauty and intelligence. How trying it is to live among these stupid little creatures! With all the rain we've been having of late the floods will soon be here, and then I'll allow myself to be swept down into the big river and out of this little pool. Then I'll be able to mix with my equals – the other big fish.'

When he told the other fish in the pool, they all agreed what a splendid idea it sounded. With solemn faces, the older fish congratulated him, saying how clever he was to think of such an idea.

There followed more days of heavy rains and, sure enough, the floods arrived. The waters swept over the little pool and, while most of the fish sheltered in the bottom of the pool, the big fish rose to the top and allowed the waters to sweep him downstream to the river. Once there he noticed how different the water tasted, and how much larger the rocks and weeds were. He sighed with anticipation of the good life that lay ahead.

He was resting for a few moments beside a large rock when he became aware of the water swirling behind him. Four of five fish, much bigger than he, passed over his head. 'Out of the way, little fellow! Don't you know this is our hunting ground?' they exclaimed harshly, as they drove him away. He escaped into a clump of thick, tangly weed. Anxiously he peered out from time to time, not having expected this so soon after his arrival. 'They obviously didn't realise who I was,' he comforted

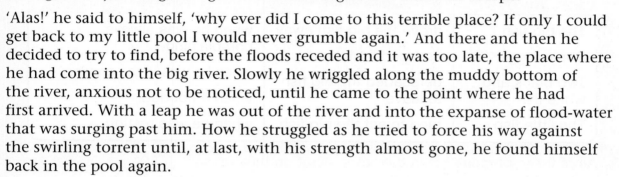

himself, somewhat uncertainly. Presently two large black and white fish came rushing straight for him, with their fearful jaws open wide. They would surely have devoured him had he not wedged himself into a crevice in the bank, just out of their reach.

All day long he dared not move, but when night came he gingerly swam out into the black water, hoping to find some supper. Suddenly he felt a sharp nip in his tail. It was a large tiger-fish, also looking for its supper. He was about to give himself up for lost when a massive dark object (a canoe – though the fish didn't know this) passed overhead, distracting the tiger-fish just long enough for the little big fish to effect his escape.

'Alas!' he said to himself, 'why ever did I come to this terrible place? If only I could get back to my little pool I would never grumble again.' And there and then he decided to try to find, before the floods receded and it was too late, the place where he had come into the big river. Slowly he wriggled along the muddy bottom of the river, anxious not to be noticed, until he came to the point where he had first arrived. With a leap he was out of the river and into the expanse of flood-water that was surging past him. How he struggled as he tried to force his way against the swirling torrent until, at last, with his strength almost gone, he found himself back in the pool again.

There he lay – panting. Too tired to move, he looked around at the familiar landmarks. 'If only I'd known what the big river was like I would never have left the safety, comfort and friendship of our pool.'

The tiny fish continued to play and splash all around him, but never again did the big fish complain or say he was too grand to live among them – even though he may still have thought so!

Senegalese folk story

Do you remember?

Write a sentence to answer each question.

1. Where did the big fish live?
2. Who else lived with him in the pool?
3. Why did the big fish want to leave the pool?
4. When was he able to leave the pool?
5. What happened when he first reached the river?
6. Who bit him in the tail?
7. Did he stay in the river? Why?
8. Was he glad to be back in the pool?

More to think about

1. Write a sentence to answer each question.
    a) Why does the author describe the pool as "a happy pool"?
    b) If it was a happy pool, why did the big fish want to leave?
    c) How did the older fish in the pool encourage the big fish to leave?
    d) Why did the big fish think, "They obviously didn't realise who I was" when the fish in the river attacked him?
    e) Why, after he returned to the pool, did the big fish not complain about the small fish when they played and splashed?

2. Choose a phrase from each box to make four sentences about the story.

Who?	Does what?	When?
The big fish	drove the big fish away	when he was always complaining.
Some bigger fish	escaped into the river	when he was in the crevice.
Two black and white fish	persuaded the big fish to leave	when it flooded.
The little fish	tried to eat the big fish	when he was resting.

3. All of these phrases are in the story. What do they mean?
    a) kept himself to himself
    b) please stop the commotion
    c) the big fish's constant gripes
    d) their fearful jaws
    e) he gingerly swam out
    f) to effect his escape

Now try these

1. Write a brief version of the story using only five sentences.

2. Have you ever met a person like the big fish?
    In what ways does the big fish remind you of them?

3. This story contains a moral (or message) for humans.
    Write what you think it is.

Views of Winter

These two poems give very different views of winter.

Winter Morning

Winter is the king of showmen,
Turning tree stumps into snowmen
And houses into birthday cakes
And spreading sugar over lakes.
Smooth and clean and frosty white,
The world looks good enough to bite.
That's the season to be young,
Catching snowflakes on your tongue.
Snow is snowy when it's snowing,
I'm sorry it's slushy when it's going.

Ogden Nash

Winter in a Wheelchair

Icy tyres scratch my hands,
Fingers stiff and numb,
My independence melts away,
Like a snowman in the sun.

Alone in my chair,
I watch the children play and yell,
This winter wonderland of snow,
For me is winter hell.

Emma Barnes

Do you remember?

Copy this paragraph. Fill each gap.

The poems were written by ____1____ and ____2____. They are both about ____3____. In 'Winter Morning' winter is ____4____, but for the writer of 'Winter in a Wheelchair' it is ____5____. In 'Winter Morning', the poet imagines ____6____ are turned into birthday cakes. He likes the snow best when it is ____7____ and ____8____ and frosty white, and is sorry when it's ____9____. Emma Barnes' poem reminds us that icy tyres ____10____ your hands, and you can feel very ____11____ in a chair as you watch other children ____12____.

More to think about

1. Make a list of the reasons given in 'Winter Morning' to enjoy winter.

2. Make a list of the reasons why it is hard to enjoy winter, according to 'Winter in a Wheelchair'.

3. Explain in your own words what is meant in 'Winter Morning' by:
   a) Winter is the king of showmen.
   b) The world looks good enough to bite.
   c) That's the season to be young.

4. Explain in your own words what is meant in 'Winter in a Wheelchair' by:
   a) Icy tyres scratch my hands.
   b) My independence melts away.
   c) This winter wonderland of snow, For me is winter hell.

Now try these

1. Which of the poems did you prefer? Give your reasons.

2. Imagine that you are the child in Emma's poem.
   a) Make a list of other things that children enjoy but, for you in a wheelchair, are difficult or impossible to do.
   b) Write a letter to a relative about when you were invited to go out for a day with a friend's family, and what happened when part of the day was spent at a huge funfair. Write about your feelings, as well as what you did.

3. Write a poem about winter from your point of view. Think about what it looks like and how it makes you feel.

Wild Swans

Jung Chang was born in Yibin, Sichuan Province in China. She wrote *Wild Swans*, partly as her autobiography and partly as a biography describing the lives of her mother and grandmother.

In the autumn of 1958, when I was six, I started going to a primary school about twenty minutes walk from home, mostly along muddy cobbled back alleys. Every day on my way to and from school, I screwed up my eyes to search every inch of ground for broken nails, rusty cogs, and any other metal objects that had been trodden into the mud between the cobbles. These were for feeding into furnaces to produce steel, which was my major occupation. Yes, at the age of six, I was involved in steel production, and had to compete with my schoolmates at handing in the most scrap iron. All around me uplifting music blared from loudspeakers, and there were banners, posters, and huge slogans painted on the walls proclaiming 'Long Live the Great Leap Forward!' and 'Everybody, Make Steel!' Although I did not fully understand why, I knew that Chairman Mao had ordered the nation to make a lot of steel. In my school, crucible-like vats had replaced some of our cooking woks and were sitting on the giant stoves in the kitchen. All our scrap iron was fed into them, including

the old woks, which had now been broken to bits. The stoves were kept permanently lit – until they melted down. Our teachers took turns feeding firewood into them around the clock, and stirring the scraps in the vats with a huge spoon. We did not have many lessons, as the teachers were too preoccupied with the vats. So were the older, teenage children. The rest of us were organised to clean the teachers' apartments and babysit for them.

I remember visiting a hospital once with some other children to see one of our teachers who had been seriously burned when molten iron had splashed onto her arms. Doctors and nurses in white coats were rushing around frantically. There was a furnace on the hospital grounds, and they had to feed logs into it all the time, even when they were performing operations, and right through the night.

Shortly before I started going to school, my family had moved from the old vicarage into a special compound, which was the centre of government for the province. A huge furnace was erected in the parking lot. At night the sky was lit up, and the noise of the crowds around the furnace could be heard 300 yards away in my room. My family's woks went into this furnace, together with all our cast-iron cooking utensils. We did not suffer from their loss, as we did not need them anymore. No private cooking was allowed now, and everybody had to eat in the canteen. The furnaces were insatiable. Gone was my parents' bed, a soft, comfortable one with iron springs. Gone also were the iron railings from the city pavements, and anything else that was iron. I hardly saw my parents for months. They often did not come home at all, as they had to make sure the temperature in their office furnaces never dropped.

It was at this time that Mao gave full vent to his half-baked dream … and ordered steel output to be doubled in one year – from 5.35 million tons in 1957 to 10.7 million in 1958. But instead of trying to expand the proper steel industry with skilled workers, he decided to get the whole population to take part. It was officially estimated that nearly 100 million peasants were pulled out of agricultural work and into steel production. They had been the labour force producing much of the country's food.

Jung Chang

Do you remember?

Copy and finish these sentences.

1. At the age of six, Jung's walk to school was …
2. In 1958 the Chinese leader was …
3. Jung didn't have many lessons because …
4. One of Jung's teachers was in hospital because …
5. Jung's family did not have many cooking utensils because …
6. Many of the steel workers had been …

More to think about

1. Write a sentence to answer each question.
   a) Why was Jung Chang so anxious to collect metal waste on her way to school?
   b) Why was loud music being played in the streets?
   c) What clues are there in the passage that everyone was very anxious to make as much steel as possible?
   d) What did the pupils do to help their school reach the targets for steel production?
   e) Make a list of the ways that the home lives of ordinary Chinese families were disrupted in the push to produce steel?

2. From the way each of these words or phrases is used in the passage, say what you think it means. Use a dictionary to help you.
   a) uplifting music
   b) huge slogans
   c) crucible-like vats
   d) molten iron
   e) insatiable
   f) half-baked dream

Now try these

1. Do you think Jung Chang thought that Chairman Mao's ideas for running the country were sensible? Give your reasons.

2. Would you have wanted to live in China in the 1950s?
   Describe the main ways Jung's daily life was different from yours today.

3. An autobiography is written in the first person, using the pronouns 'I' and 'we'. Rewrite the first paragraph in the third person, using 'she' and 'they' to describe Jung's experiences.

Barack Obama: A Biography

Barack Hussein Obama was born on 4th August 1961, in Honolulu, Hawaii. Obama's mother, Ann Dunham, grew up in Kansas, U.S.A. and his father, Barack Obama, Sr., was born in Nyanza Province, Kenya. They met at the University of Hawaii and married on 2nd February, 1961.

Obama's parents separated when he was only two years old, and later divorced. Obama, Sr. went on to Harvard University to pursue further studies, and then returned to Kenya in 1965. In 1966, Barack's mother married Lolo Soetoro and the family moved to Indonesia. Several incidents in Indonesia left Barack's mother afraid for her son's safety and education so, at the age of ten, he was sent back to Hawaii to live with his maternal grandparents. His mother and half-sister later joined them.

While living with his grandparents, Obama was given a place in the highly regarded Punahou Academy, where he excelled in basketball. As one of only three black students at the school, Obama became conscious of racism and what it meant to be African-American. He later described how he struggled to reconcile other people's perceptions of his multiracial heritage with his own sense of himself. "I began to notice there was nobody like me in the Christmas catalogues ... and that Santa was a white man," he said.

Obama was also unhappy because of the absence of his father. His father wrote to him regularly but, though he travelled around the world on official business for Kenya, he visited only once. Obama, Jr. was 22 years old when he received the news that his father had died in a car accident in Kenya.

Obama attended Columbia University and found New York's racial tension inescapable. He attended Harvard Law School and chose to practise civil-rights law in Chicago. He represented victims of housing and employment discrimination and worked on voting-rights legislation. He married Michelle Robinson, a fellow attorney.

Eventually he was elected to the Illinois state senate. His district included some of the poorest ghettos on the South Side.

In 2004, Obama was elected to the U.S. Senate as a Democrat. He gained national attention by giving a rousing and well-received speech at the Democratic National Convention. In 2008 he ran for President and won. In January 2009, he was sworn in as the 44th President of the United States, the first African-American ever elected to that position.

Do you remember?

1. Find the grid reference to answer each question about Barack Obama. The first one has been done to help you.

	A	B	C
1	Hawaii	Kenya	Ann Dunham
2	January 2009	basketball	August 1961
3	law	Michelle	Illinois

   a) When was he born? C2
   b) Where was he born?
   c) What is the name of his wife?
   d) What was his mother's name?
   e) What did he study at Harvard?
   f) When was he inaugurated as President of the United States?
   g) What sport was he very good at?
   h) Where was his father born?
   i) What state did he represent in the senate?

2. Use a dictionary to write the meaning of each of these words.
   a) maternal
   b) excelled
   c) reconcile
   d) perceptions
   e) inescapable
   f) legislation
   g) ghettos
   h) rousing

More to think about

1. What evidence is there in the life of Barack's father to suggest that his son might inherit the drive and ability to achieve great things?

2. Barack's mother would have been sad to send her son away when she lived in Indonesia with her new husband, but it had some important effects on his life. What were these?

3. How did being one of only three African-American students at school feel to Barack? Was it a good experience?

4. Did Barack's separation from his father worry him? Use quotations from the passage to support your answer.

Now try these

1. Turn the information into 'Quick facts' and 'Trivia'. Remember to use bullet points and short sentences.

2. Have you ever been in a situation where you have been rejected by your friends or those around you? Describe what happened and how you felt.

3. Why was Barack Obama's election to the Presidency so important to so many people both in the United States and elsewhere?

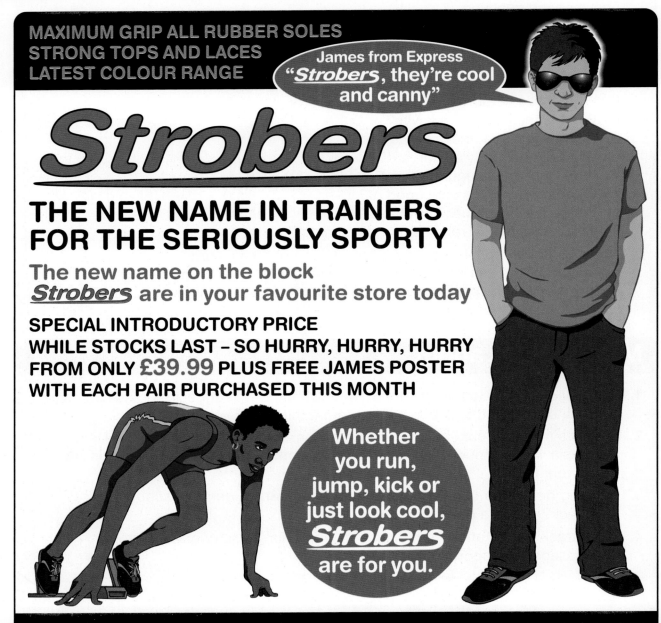

FOR SALE – STROBERS
New range of sports shoe now on sale
PRICE £40 – £70 PER PAIR

Do you remember?

Write a sentence to answer each question.

1. What are Strobers?
2. How much would a pair of Strobers cost you?
3. Where can you buy them?
4. What are the soles made of?
5. Who is promoting the shoes?
6. What extra gift do you get if you buy a pair this month?
7. How long is the special offer price available?

More to think about

1. There are two advertisements for Strobers.
   a) Which one is more likely to attract your attention? Give your reasons.
   b) What features described are the ones that would most appeal to you?

2. Advertisers want us to feel good about their products.
   a) Which words in the top advertisement are 'feel good' words?
   b) Which words in the advertisement appeal to sporty people?
   c) Which words in the advertisement appeal to people who want to look good?
   d) Which words actually describe the shoes?

3. What other devices have been used to persuade you to go out and buy Strobers?

4. What sort of people do you think the big advertisement is aimed at?
   Would this sort of advertisement encourage you to think about buying Strobers next time you need new trainers? Explain your answer.

Now try these

1. Why do you think that James, from the new pop group Express, has been chosen to be on an advertisement for sports shoes?

2. Give your opinion on these statements:
   a) If you buy something because someone famous has their name on it, it is certain to be good.
   b) If you don't buy immediately when an advertisement with an introductory offer appears, the product is certain to cost more later.
   c) It is sensible for the company to use the word *Strobers* in this font every time.

3. Find three advertisements in magazines. Write about how well you think each of the advertisements does its job. Give your reasons.

4. Write and design your own advertisement for a new range of mountain bikes. Think of a good brand name, and carefully choose the 'selling' words you are going to use. Finally, make a strong, eye-catching and colourful design.

The Railway Children

'Please 'm,' said Ruth, 'the Master wants you to just step into the study. He looks like the dead, mum; I think he's had bad news. You'd best prepare yourself for the worst, 'm – p'raps it's a death in the family or a bank busted or –'

'That'll do Ruth,' said Mother gently, 'you can go.'

Then Mother went into the library. There was more talking. Then the bell rang again, and Ruth fetched a cab. The children heard boots go out and down the steps. The cab drove away, and the front door shut. Then Mother came in. Her dear face was as white as her lace collar, and her eyes looked very big and shining. Her mouth looked just like a line of pale red – her lips were thin and not their proper shape at all.

'It's bedtime,' she said. 'Ruth will put you to bed.'

'But you promised we should sit up late tonight because Father's come home,' said Phyllis.

'Father's been called away – on business,' said Mother. 'Come, darlings, go at once.'

They kissed her and went. Roberta lingered to give Mother an extra hug and to whisper:

'It wasn't bad news, Mammy, was it? Is anyone dead – or –'

'Nobody's dead – no,' said Mother, and she almost seemed to push Roberta away. 'I can't tell you anything tonight, my pet. Go, dear; go *now*.'

So Roberta went.

Ruth brushed the girls' hair and helped them to undress. (Mother almost always did this herself.) When she had turned down the gas and left them she found Peter, still dressed, waiting on the stairs.

'I say, Ruth, what's up?' he asked.

'Don't ask me no questions and I won't tell you no lies,' the red-headed Ruth replied. 'You'll know soon enough.'

Late that night Mother came up and kissed all three children as they lay asleep. But Roberta was the only one whom the kiss woke, and she lay mousey-still, and said nothing.

'If Mother doesn't want us to know she's been crying,' she said to herself as she heard through the dark the catching of her mother's breath, 'we won't know it. That's all.'

When they came down to breakfast the next morning, Mother had already gone out.

'To London,' Ruth said, and left them to their breakfast.

It was nearly seven before she came in, looking so ill and tired that the children felt they could not ask her any questions. She sank into an arm-chair. Phyllis took the long pins out of her hat, while Roberta took off her gloves, and Peter unfastened her walking-shoes and fetched her soft velvety slippers for her.

When she had had a cup of tea, and Roberta had put eau-de-Cologne on her poor head that ached, Mother said:

'Now, my darlings, I want to tell you something. Those men last night did bring very bad news, and Father will be away for some time. I am very worried about it, and I want you all to help me, and not to make things harder for me.'

'As if we would!' said Roberta, holding Mother's hand against her face.

'You can help me very much,' said Mother, 'by being good and happy and not quarrelling when I'm away' – Roberta and Peter exchanged guilty glances – 'for I shall have to be away a good deal.'

'We won't quarrel. Indeed we won't,' said everyone. And meant it, too.

'Then,' Mother went on, 'I want you not to ask me any questions about this trouble; and not to ask anybody else any questions.'

Peter cringed and shuffled his boots on the carpet.

'You'll promise this, too, won't you?' said Mother.

'I did ask Ruth,' said Peter, suddenly. 'I'm very sorry, but I did.'

'And what did she say?'

'She said I should know soon enough.'

'It isn't necessary for you to know anything about it,' said Mother; 'it's about business, and you never do understand business, do you?'

'No,' said Roberta, 'is it something to do with Government?' For Father was in a Government Office.

'Yes,' said Mother. 'Now it's bedtime, my darlings. And don't *you* worry. It'll all come right in the end.'

'Then don't *you* worry either, Mother,' said Phyllis, 'and we'll all be as good as gold.'

Mother sighed and kissed them.

E Nesbit

Do you remember?

Copy these sentences. Choose the correct ending to finish each sentence.

1. The maid's name was
   a) Rebecca.
   b) Ruth.
   c) Roberta.

2. In the family there were
   a) two children.
   b) three children.
   c) four children.

3. Mother said Father had to go away
   a) on business.
   b) to see her mother.
   c) to the doctor.

4. Next day Mother went to
   a) Glasgow.
   b) London.
   c) Cardiff.

5. She arrived home at
   a) six o'clock.
   b) seven o'clock.
   c) eight o'clock.

More to think about

1. Write a sentence to answer each question.
   a) What clues can you find to suggest that the family was rich?
   b) How can you tell from the passage that the story was written over 100 years ago?
   c) How well did Roberta and Peter usually get on with each other?
   d) When her mother came to kiss the children goodnight, why did Roberta pretend that she was asleep?
   e) Why do you think that Mother didn't want to talk about where their father had gone?

2. Write three sentences about each of these characters:
   a) Ruth   b) Mother
   c) Peter   d) Roberta.

3. Find these phrases in the passage, and explain what they mean in your own words.
   a) "He looks like the dead, mum"
   b) The children heard boots go out and down the steps.
   c) Her dear face was as white as her lace collar
   d) Roberta lingered
   e) she lay mousey-still
   f) she sank into an arm-chair

Now try these

1. In a few sentences, summarise what happens in the passage.

2. This passage occurs near the beginning of *The Railway Children*. Did you enjoy the passage? Would you like to read the rest of the story? Give your reasons.

3. Why do you think Father went away? Pretend you are Mother and write how you would explain the reason to the children.

Gulliver's Travels

Lemuel Gulliver, a ship's doctor, is the only survivor to reach the shore when his boat goes down in a great storm in 1699. Exhausted, he falls into a deep sleep.

I must have slept for a long time, for the sun had just begun to rise above the horizon when I awoke. I tried to stand up but found to my astonishment that I could not move. My hands and feet and even my hair seemed to be fastened to the ground. The sun was getting hotter. Then I was horrified to feel some small creatures moving along my left leg and up to my chest. Straining to lift my head a little, I peered down and saw a tiny human creature not much bigger than my middle finger. He was followed by about forty more of the same kind.

I was so astonished that I roared aloud. With this they all ran back in fright, and some even fell off. However, they soon returned and one climbed up to where he could get a full sight of my face.

"*Hekinah Degul!*" he called out but, although I've studied several other languages besides my native English, I could not understand what he meant.

With a violent pull, I managed to break a few of the strings that bound my left hand. I then tried to catch some of the annoying little creatures, but I could not – they ran away far too quickly.

Then one of them cried aloud, "*Tolgo Phonac!*" In an instance I felt my left hand and my face pierced with hundreds of tiny arrows. Although it was very painful, I decided not to anger my tiny captors further. I lay still and tried to think about how to get free later, when they had all gone away and left me alone.

After a little while, I heard some knocking near my right ear and the sound of a great crowd. Turning my head as far as I could, I saw that some of the tiny people were building a tower about half a metre high. Now one little man, who seemed to be important, climbed up to the top of it and made a long speech, not a word of which I could understand. He said the word *"Lilliput"* several times, however, and I guessed that this might be the name of the place I was in. He looked quite friendly, and since I was very hungry, I put my finger to my mouth to indicate this.

Before long, about a hundred inhabitants set ladders against my sides and climbed up and walked towards my mouth, carrying little baskets of food: miniature legs of lamb, tiny roasted turkeys and sides of beef. They were deliciously cooked, but three of them together made scarcely a mouthful for me.

Then someone called out, *"Peplum selam."* At this, they loosened the cords that bound me a little, so I was able to turn on my side. Before I knew it I was fast asleep. Only later did I discover that their doctors had put a sleeping potion into my food.

Jonathan Swift

Do you remember?

1. Read these sentences about the story.
   Write 'true', 'false' or 'can't tell' for each one.
   a) It was close to midday when Gulliver awoke on the beach.
   b) Gulliver counted about 40 little people to begin with.
   c) Gulliver realised that they were speaking Italian.
   d) He thought the place was called Lilliput as this was a name the little people used.
   e) The little people refused to feed Gulliver.
   f) Gulliver never did realise that he had been drugged by the little people.

2. Write a sentence to answer each question.
   a) How did the little people restrain Gulliver?
   b) What happened when Gulliver gave a great shout?
   c) Why did he decide it was better not to try to escape?
   d) What was Gulliver given to eat?
   e) Why were the little people not worried about undoing some of his ropes?

More to think about

1. Write a sentence to say how we can tell that:
   a) Gulliver woke early in the morning.
   b) the sheep and cattle on Lilliput were also very small.
   c) the little people were good cooks.

2. In the passage, find the following words. Write another word that could be used in place of each word without altering the meaning.
   a) astonishment
   b) roared
   c) indicate
   d) peered
   e) violent
   f) inhabitants

3. Write a brief summary, using no more than 40 words, giving all the key facts of the passage.

Now try these

1. From what you can tell from the passage, write a few sentences describing the sort of person you imagine Gulliver to have been.
   Think particularly about his personality, and the way he reacted in a crisis.

2. Imagine you are one of the little people who found Gulliver washed up on the beach. Write about your first reaction, how you felt and what you did.

3. Individually, the Lilliputians could not have restrained the huge outsider, but working together they did. Write about something you have achieved by working with other people that would have been impossible to do by yourself.

The Little Match Girl

It was snowing and the wind grew cold as darkness fell over the city. It was New Year's Eve. In the gathering gloom a little girl with bare feet padded through the streets. She had been wearing her mother's slippers when she left home, but they were far too big, and she had lost them while hurrying across a busy road. One of them was nowhere to be found, and a boy ran off with the other. So now her bare feet were mottled blue and red with the bitter cold.

In her old apron the little girl carried bundles of matches which her father had sent her out to sell, but all day long nobody had bought a single match from her. Cold and hungry, she made her weary way through the city. Brilliant lights streamed from the windows of big houses, where blazing fires crackled merrily in the hearth, and the smell of roast goose hung on the air, for it was New Year's Eve.

The little girl crouched down in a corner between two houses. She drew her knees up to her chest, but this seemed to make her even colder. She was afraid to go home, for she had sold nothing the whole day! Not a penny had she earned, and her father would surely be angry with her. But it was just as cold at home, for the wind whistled through the cracks in the walls and floorboards.

How wonderful it would be to light a match! All she had to do was take one out of the bundle, strike it on the wall, and warm her fingers at the flame. She drew out a match and struck it. How it sparkled and gleamed! How the flames leapt and the flames danced! It seemed to the little girl as if she were sitting at an enormous iron stove with brass ornaments on it. She stretched out her frozen feet to warm them – and the flame went out. Gone was the wonderful stove, and there she sat in the snow with the burnt-out match smoking between her fingers.

She struck another. The match flared up, making a new circle of brightness. The light fell on the stone wall, which immediately became as transparent as gauze. She found herself looking into a cosy room, where a table stood spread with a white linen tablecloth and set with silver, while in the middle steamed an enormous roast goose. The goose leapt out of the dish towards her – and the match went out. She saw nothing but the cold, grey wall before her.

Once again she struck a match, and found herself sitting at the foot of a magnificent Christmas tree. Thousands of tiny candles twinkled on the tips of the green branches, and brilliant paper streamers and tinsel hung down to the floor. The little girl stretched both her hands towards it – and the match went out. The candles seemed to climb higher and higher, until she saw that they were the cold, bright stars above her. One of them fell across the wintry sky, drawing a long fiery tail behind it. Someone must be dying, she thought, for her old grandmother, who had always been so kind to her, had said, 'Whenever you see a falling star, you know that a soul is on its way to God!'

She struck another match. It threw a warm circle of light all round her, and within the bright circle stood her grandmother, smiling gently down on her.

'Oh, Grandmother,' cried the poor girl, 'take me with you please! I know I shall never see you again once the match burns out. You will vanish, just as the warm stove, the roast goose, and the beautiful Christmas tree did!' Quickly she struck the remaining matches, one after the other, for she did not want her grandmother to disappear.

Never had her grandmother looked so kind. She gathered the little girl into her arms and swept her up to heaven. How bright everything was! Here she felt neither cold, nor hunger, nor fear – for they were with God.

Early next day the people found the little match-girl huddled against the wall, the spent matches scattered about her. She was dead, but there was a smile of happiness on her lips.

'Poor soul, she was trying to warm herself,' the people said, but no one guessed what beautiful things the match-girl had seen by the light of her matches, nor how happy she was with her grandmother that beautiful New Year's morning.

Hans Christian Andersen

Do you remember?

Copy this paragraph. Fill each gap.

The little ___1___ was feeling very ___2___. Her ___3___ had sent her out to sell ___4___. She was afraid to go ___5___, for her father would be angry. How wonderful it would be to ___6___ a match! The ___7___ leapt and danced. She imagined it was an iron ___8___. She stretched out her ___9___ to warm them, but the flame went ___10___.

More to think about

1. As the little girl struck the matches she thought she saw an enormous iron stove with brass ornaments, her grandmother, an enormous roast goose and a Christmas tree with thousands of tiny, twinkling candles.
   Write in your book the order in which these appeared to her.

2. Write a sentence to answer each question.
   a) How can you tell that the little match girl's family were very poor?
   b) Why would her father have been cross if she had gone home without selling the matches?
   c) Did she usually light matches from the bundles? Explain the reason for your answer.
   d) What do you think caused the little girl to imagine such vivid scenes as she struck each match?
   e) To which of her relations had the little girl felt particularly close?
   f) Why did she have a smile on her lips when she was found dead?

3. Describe in your own words the place where the story of the little match girl is set.

Now try these

1. Did you enjoy this story by Hans Christian Andersen? Give your reasons.

2. The little match girl was frightened to go home.
   a) How do you think her parents were feeling when she didn't return?
   b) Do you think she was right to stay out?

3. Have you ever been afraid to admit to something?
   Describe how you felt and what happened in the end.

34

Climate Change, What Climate Change?

Hi Grandad

23 Jun

You know I told you about this project about climate change I've got to do at school – well I'm getting a bit confused. One of my friends said it's all made up by journalists who like a good story to sell their newspapers and that the Earth isn't really warming up. He says it was really cold last winter.

Josh x

My dear Josh

23 Jun

I know we had a cold winter, but that was just in our country and in one year – but we need to look at our planet Earth overall and over several years.

Think of it like this. What happens when you go into a greenhouse on a sunny day? It's hot, isn't it? That's because the glass in the greenhouse traps the heat from the sun. This carbon dioxide gas (and some others as well) that is produced when we burn oil and coal does the same in the Earth's atmosphere. That's why we call them greenhouse gases! The atmosphere acts like glass in a greenhouse. But without them, we'd freeze, so we certainly need some, but not too much of them or the planet warms more than it should.

So, with all the gases being pumped out of cars, aircraft, power stations and so on, we must be emitting more greenhouse gases and so climate change must be taking place.

Grandad x

Yesterday

Thanks for your email Grandad, but my friend Pete, whose dad works for an oil company, says that the temperatures on Earth have always gone up and down. That's why we had an ice age with woolly mammoths and polar bears roaming around. And now it's warm.

Josh x

Hi Josh
Pete has a point but the next ice age isn't due here for another 10,000 years. At the rate the Earth's climate and oceans are warming, the ice in the Arctic and Antarctic will have melted so much that many low-lying places will have flooded already. So we can't hang about waiting for 10,000 years, can we?
Grandad x

10.30

My dear Josh
I've been thinking more about the email you sent yesterday. Global warming? Phooey! There are some people, like Pete's dad, who say it is not happening. Can you think who some of these might be? You guessed it! Those who use lots of fuel, who make things like cars that use lots of fuel, or actually get the fuel out of the earth – that's heavy industry, car makers and the oil, gas and coal companies. This is what people call 'vested interest'. These are people who depend on other people using lots of fuel if they are to continue making money. It's not surprising that they don't think there is any climate change. But it doesn't make them right, does it! It makes me cross!
Grandad x

16.42

You're right Grandad. I bet people from low-lying countries aren't saying we needn't be worried!
Josh x

17.23

My dear Josh
Quite so, and as your grandfather I'm worried for you and all my other lovely grandchildren. I fear there's worse to come. People who study the Earth's climate have found that as it warms up, the weather is going to get more violent and unpredictable. Hurricanes, for example, will become more powerful – a big worry for people living in the south of the United States and in the tropical Pacific or Indian Ocean areas, like the Philippines and Bangladesh. Deserts are increasing and places where lots of the Earth's food is grown, like the Great Plains of North America, will get drier. Rain will be heavier in other parts of the world so there will be more floods. These things have already started to happen.
So even if we think there might be some doubts about some of the science, I don't think we should wait to find out, do you?
Grandad x

17.41

No, Grandad, I certainly don't think we should wait!
Thanks for your help with this.
Josh x

Do you remember?

Write a sentence to answer each question.

1. Why does Josh's friend think many journalists write about climate change?
2. Give one reason why Pete thinks the Earth isn't getting warmer.
3. Why is carbon dioxide called a greenhouse gas?
4. Where do many of the greenhouse gases come from?
5. Where does Pete's father work?
6. When is the next ice age due to happen?

More to think about

Write some sentences to answer each question.

1. Why do more people in Europe and America than in Africa and Asia seem less worried about climate change?
2. What are the main arguments put forward by Grandad suggesting that climate change needs to be taken seriously?
3. What would be the implications if we had no greenhouse gases in our atmosphere?
4. What is meant by "vested interests"?
5. Why is it potentially worrying if there is decreasing rainfall in the Great Plains of North America?
6. Explain how climate change can result in less rain in some countries but flooding in low-lying regions, such as areas of Bangladesh.

Now try these

1. Write the conversation that might occur if Grandad was to meet Pete's dad. It has been started to help you. Remember to use the correct punctuation.

   "Hi there, I'm Josh's grandad. You must be Pete's father."
   "Yes, I am and I'm pleased to meet you."

2. Make a poster either in favour or against the building of a new coal-fired power station near your home.

3. Use the internet or reference books to research the arguments for or against whether the Earth's climate is changing and whether this matters. Use your research to help you write a speech that you could read to your class arguing one way or the other.

The BFG

Sophie was terrified when the Big Friendly Giant (BFG) snatched her from her bed. Imagine her relief when she realised he was not a 'cannybull' who ate humans, but a reluctant eater of an unpleasant vegetable, snozzcumber. But whatever was the BFG pouring into his trumpet and blowing through children's bedrooms as they slept?

The Big Friendly Giant put the suitcase on the ground. He bent down low so that his enormous face was close to Sophie's. 'From now on, we keep as still as winky little mices,' he whispered.

Sophie nodded. The misty vapour swirled around her. It made her cheeks damp and left dewdrops in her hair.

The BFG opened the suitcase and took out several empty glass jars. He set them on the ground, with their screw tops removed. Then he stood up very straight. His head was now high up in the swirling mist and it kept disappearing, then appearing again. He was holding the long net in his right hand.

Sophie, staring upwards, saw through the mist that his colossal ears were beginning to swivel out from his head. They began waving gently to and fro.

Suddenly the BFG pounced. He leaped high in the air and swung the net through the mist with a great swishing sweep of his arm. 'Got him!' he cried. 'A jar! A jar! Quick quick quick! Sophie picked up a jar and held it up to him. He grabbed hold of it. He lowered the net. Very carefully he tipped something absolutely invisible from the net into the jar. He dropped the net and swiftly clapped one hand over the jar. 'The top!' he whispered. 'The jar top quick!' Sophie picked up a jar top and handed it to him. He screwed it on tight and the jar was closed. The BFG was very excited. He held the jar close to one ear and listened intently.

'It's a winksquiffler!' he whispered with a thrill in his voice. 'It's...it's...it's...it's even better. It's a phizzwizard! It's a golden phizzwizard!'

Sophie stared at him.

'Oh my, oh my!' he said, holding the jar in front of him. 'This will be giving some little tottler a very happy night when I is blowing it in!'

'Is it really a good one?' Sophie asked.

'A *good one*?' he cried. 'It's a golden phizzwizard! It is not often I is getting one of these!' He handed the jar to Sophie and said 'Please be still as a star fish now. I is thinking there may be a whole swarm of phizzwizards up there today. And do kindly stop breathing. You is terribly noisy down there.'

I haven't moved a muscle,' Sophie said.

'Then don't,' the BFG answered sharply. Once again he stood up tall in the mist, holding his net at the ready. Then came the long silence, the waiting, the listening, and at last, with surprising suddenness came the leap and the swish of the net.

'Another jar!' he cried. 'Quick quick quick!'

When the second dream was safely in the jar and the top was screwed down, the BFG held it to his ear.

'Oh *no*!' he cried. 'Oh mince my maggots! Oh swipe my swoggles!'

'What's the matter?' Sophie asked.

'It's a trogglehumper!' he shouted. His voice was filled with fury and anguish. 'Oh, save our solos!' he cried, 'deliver us from weasels! The devil is dancing on my dibbler!'

'What are you talking about?' Sophie said. The BFG was getting more distressed every moment.

'Oh, bash my eyebones!' he cried, waving the jar in the air. 'I come all this way to get lovely golden dreams and what is I catching?'

'What *are* you catching?' Sophie said.

'I is catching a frightful trogglehumper!' he cried. 'This is a *bad bad dream*! It is worse than a bad dream! It is a *nightmare*!'

'I is never never letting it go!' the BFG cried. 'If I do, then some poor little tottler will be having the most curdbloodling time! This one is a real kicksy bogthumper! I is exploding it as soon as I get home!'

'Nightmares are horrible,' Sophie said. 'I had one once and I woke up sweating all over.'

'With this one you would be waking up *screaming* all over!' the BFG said. 'This one would make your teeth stand on end! If this one got inside you, your blood would be freezing to icicles and your skin would be creeping across the floor!'

'Is it as bad as that?'

'It's worse!' cried the BFG. 'This is a really whoppsy grobswitcher!'

'You said it was a trogglehumper,' Sophie told him.

'It is a trogglehumper!' cried the exasperated BFG.
'But it is also a *bogthumper* and a *grobswitcher*! It is all three
riddled into one! Oh, I is so glad I is clutching it tight.
Ah, you wicked beastie, you!' he cried, holding up
the jar and staring into it. 'Never more is you going to be
bunkdoodling the poor little human-beaney tottlers!'

Sophie, who was also staring into the glass jar, cried out,
'I can see it! There's something in there!'

'Of course there is something in there,' the BFG said.
'You is looking at a frightsome trogglehumper.'

'But you told me dreams were invisible.'

'They is always invisible until they is *captured*,' the BFG told her.

'After that they is losing a little of their invisibility. We is seeing this one very clearly.'

Inside the jar Sophie could see the faint outline of something that looked like
a mixture between a blob of gas and a bubble of jelly. It was moving violently,
thrashing against the sides of the jar and forever changing shape.

'It's wiggling all over the place!' Sophie cried. 'It's fighting to get out! It's bashing
itself to bits!'

'The nastier the dream, the angrier it is getting when it is in prison,' the BFG said.
'It is the same as with wild animals. If an animal is very fierce and you is putting it
in a cage, it will make a tremendous rumpledumpus. If it is a nice animal, like
a cockatootloo or a fogglefrump, it will sit quietly. Dreams are exactly the same.
This one is a nasty fierce bogrotting nightmare. Just look at him splashing himself
against the glass!'

'It's quite frightening!' Sophie cried.

'I would be hating to get this one inside me on a darksome night,' the BFG said.

'So would I!' Sophie said.

The BFG started putting the bottles back into the suitcase.

'Is that all?' Sophie asked. 'Are we going?'

'I is so upset by this trogglehumping bogthumping grobswitcher,' the BFG said,
'that I is not wishing to go on. Dream-catching is finished for today.'

Soon Sophie was back in the waistcoat pocket and the BFG was racing home as fast
as he could go. When, at last, they emerged out of the mist and came again on to
the hot yellow wasteland, all the other giants were sprawled out on the ground,
fast asleep.

Roald Dahl

Do you remember?

Write a sentence to answer each question.

1. What did the BFG have in his suitcase?
2. What was he holding in his right hand?
3. How does the author describe the BFG's ears?
4. What was the first thing he caught?
5. What sort of dream is a winksquiffler?
6. What is the difference between a winksquiffler and a phizzwizard?
7. Why did the giant ask Sophie to "kindly stop breathing"?

More to think about

1. Write a sentence to answer each question.
   a) What is a trogglehumper?
   b) What was special about the particular trogglehumper the BFG caught?
   c) How did catching the trogglehumper affect the BFG?
   d) How can you tell that the giant was probably at least ten times bigger than Sophie?
2. Write five phrases that the BFG uses to describe how frightening the trogglehumper is.

Now try these

1. The BFG was sometimes confused by certain words and phrases. Write what he should have said instead of:
   a) little mices.
   b) This will be giving some little tottler a very happy night.
   c) What is I catching?
   d) This one would make your teeth stand on end!
   e) Oh, I is so glad I is clutching it tight.
   f) the poor little human-beaney tottlers.

2. Write what each of these people might say if the BFG appeared to them:
   a) your teacher, when the BFG looks through the classroom window
   b) your mum, when you bring him home for tea
   c) the bus driver, when he tries to squeeze onto his bus
   d) the dentist, when he arrives at the surgery with a bad toothache.

3. What do you think would be the best things and worst things about being a giant? Make two lists.

4. If you were a story 'judge', how many marks out of 10 would you give the story of the BFG? Explain why you would award it this score.

Compere Lapin and Compere Tig

It was a warm sunny morning when the King visited his pool. As soon as he saw the water he knew someone had been to the pool before him, leaving it murky and dirty. The King was furious.

'O King, Compere Lapin is the culprit. It was he who visited the pool,' said one of his wise men.

'I will not have it. He must die. No one visits the pool before the King,' thundered the King.

When Compere Lapin heard what had happened, he said to his friend Compere Tig, 'There is a beautiful, cool pool in the yard. The King says you may bathe in it.' Compere Tig was flattered and delighted and went straight to the pool. But as he was coming out the King spotted him and ordered his arrest. He was put in a bag, and the bag was hung in a tree. Then the King ordered a long iron bar to be heated until it was red hot so that Compere Tig could be burnt. It took two long days for the iron to be heated. Meanwhile, Compere Lapin visited Compere Tig to make fun of him. He stood at the bottom of the tree and called, 'Tig, Tig, *ou kai bwelay*!'

Compere Tig had an idea. 'Compere Lapin, Compere Lapin! Please help me. The King has said I must marry his daughter and because I refused he has said I must die.'

When Compere Lapin heard this he decided that if he exchanged places with Compere Tig he could offer to marry the princess. Being a very greedy fellow he immediately started to think of the wonderful food and riches that would be his – not to mention the beautiful daughter of the King. He didn't stop for one moment to consider that he was being fooled, just as he had deceived his friend Compere Tig.

So he quickly untied the bag, and changed places, and Tig securely retied the bag and hauled it back into the tree.

'Goodbye Compere Lapin, *ou kai bwelay*!'

St Lucian folk story

Do you remember?

**Match these questions and answers.
Write the answers in the correct order.**

1. At what time of day did the King visit his pool?

2. What was the weather like when the King went to the pool?

3. Why was the King furious when he saw the pool?

4. Why was Compere Tig arrested?

5. Who had told Compere Tig he could swim in the pool?

Answers

- Compere Lapin had told Compere Tig that the King had said he could bathe in the pool.
- The King visited his pool in the morning.
- Compere Tig was arrested because the King later saw him in the pool.
- It was warm and sunny when the King visited the pool.
- Someone had visited the pool before him and left it murky and dirty.

More to think about

1. Write a sentence to answer each question.
   a) Who do you think was responsible for making the King's pool "murky and dirty"?
   b) Why did Compere Lapin want Compere Tig to bathe in the pool?
   c) How did he encourage Tig to go into the pool?
   d) What was Tig's reaction when Lapin suggested that he might swim in the King's pool?
   e) "*Ou kai bwelay*" is a phrase in the St Lucian dialect that appears twice in the story. What do you think it means?

2. Explain in your own words how Compere Tig persuaded Compere Lapin to change places with him.

3. Copy the words and phrases that the writer uses to encourage the reader to dislike Compere Lapin and to think he is an unpleasant character.

Now try these

1. At the end of the story it seems that Lapin is going to be very cruelly killed. Describe the sorts of feelings this makes you have for each of the characters?

2. Make up your own ending for the story. Is Lapin killed, or is it a clever trick to frighten him, or even a trick to get him to marry the King's daughter? You may have other ideas.

3. Imagine that the King comes to talk to Compere Lapin as he swings, terrified, in the bag. Write the conversation that takes place.

4. Convert the story of The King, Compere Lapin and Compere Tig into a play.

   Remember you will need to:
   - describe **the setting**
   - list the people in your play – **the characters**
   - write what is said – **the dialogue**
   - describe what the characters do – **stage directions**.

Looking Down

Anyone who has been on an aeroplane at night, waiting to come into land at an airport near a big city, will have seen the wonderful display of lights.
If you haven't, the photograph should help you to imagine what it looks like.

Night has chased away the last warm glow from the evening sky. Ribbons of orange snake and criss-cross, stretching out into the sea of blackness now engulfing the mass of twinkling lights.

A myriad of tiny lights shine from the miniature houses and the apartment blocks out in the suburbs. Each is a small haven, warming and comforting, banishing the darkness from the city.

Closer now, and the streets are alive with frenetic, insect-like activity. Creatures with glowing eyes, some red, some white, bustling busily, stopping, and bustling again along the shimmering streets and roads. Splashes of neon colour – pictures, words.

The famous monuments, floodlit, stand out, tell us where we are. The massive bulk of the Sacré Coeur cathedral, a glimpse of the Arc de Triomphe loom up towards us.

Between the medley of light and movement are swathes and ribbons of blackness where no lights, just an occasional reflection, are to be seen. What can be hidden there?

Do you remember?

Copy and finish these sentences.
1. As we come into land, there is a wonderful display of …
2. In the darkness the traffic looks like …
3. The ancient buildings can be seen because they are …
4. The "splashes of neon colour" are …
5. The "ribbons of blackness" could be …

More to think about

1. Write a sentence to answer each question.
   a) Is the aeroplane landing late in the evening or early in the morning?
   b) What are the "ribbons of orange" that stretch out "into the sea of blackness"?
   c) What "banishes the darkness from the city"?
   d) What are the creatures with glowing eyes?

2. Find a word in the passage that means:
   a) a very large number
   b) a place to shelter
   c) sending away
   d) historic buildings
   e) lit up.

3. From the way each of these words is used in the passage, say what you think it means.
   a) engulfing   d) medley
   b) bulk   e) neon
   c) frenetic   f) swathes

Now try these

1. Look at the six words below. Use a thesaurus to find other words with similar meanings that the writer might have used.
   a) engulfing   d) medley
   b) bulk   e) neon
   c) frenetic   f) swathes

2. Imagine that you are on an aeroplane, but coming into this busy city airport during the day. Describe what you can see.

3. The writing in this passage is very descriptive. What purpose do you think it was written for?

Save It!

Water levels at an all-time low

From our Environment Correspondent

The water companies have been given just three weeks to come up with plans to explain how they will respond to the current water shortage and to the long-term need to provide water for homes while, at the same time, protecting our rivers.

Leakage is the top priority. At present an average of 30% of treated water leaks away before it can be used.
Among the plans being considered is for the water companies to offer to repair leaks on customers' land free of charge.

Another way of saving water is for every home to use water more carefully. A way of encouraging this would be to introduce water meters in every household. "If people knew they had to pay for every drop of water they use," said one water company spokesman yesterday, "they would soon be far more conservation minded!"

But the government is reserving its position on water meters. Apart from the extra cost of installing the meters, they wonder about the fairness for people with large families, or those with medical conditions requiring frequent bathing, or those whose work makes them dirty.

As a third of domestic water currently goes down the toilet, reducing this could alone make a major impact on the immediate problem.

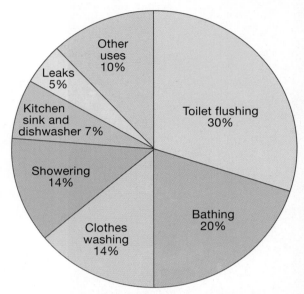

Water use in the home

A recently produced Environment Agency leaflet gives some water saving tips:
- The toilet. Placing a water-filled bottle in the cistern will help by stopping the cistern from taking in so much water as it refills.
- Showers use much less water than baths.
- Don't use washing machines or dishwashers with half loads.
- Be a water pest! Snoop for dripping taps and get them fixed.
- Use washing-up water in the garden to water the flowers and vegetables, rather than fresh water.
- Use a water butt to collect rain water for the garden.
- Turn off the tap while you are brushing your teeth.
- Don't use sprinklers unless essential.

Do you remember?

Write the correct answer to each question.

1. How long have the water companies been given to prepare their plans?
   a) one week   b) three weeks   c) three months

2. What is to be their top priority?
   a) river pollution   b) weather forecasting   c) stopping leakages

3. Why might water meters be introduced?
   a) to make more money for the companies
   b) to encourage people to use less water
   c) to stop people washing so much

4. How much domestic water is used in toilets?
   a) a quarter   b) a third   c) half

5. In what are we asked to collect rain water for the garden?
   a) a water butt   b) a watering can   c) a bucket

6. What shouldn't we use unless essential?
   a) a watering can   b) a hose   c) a sprinkler

More to think about

1. Write a sentence to answer each question.
   a) Who has asked the water companies to prepare plans?
   b) Why have they been asked to act urgently?
   c) Why might it help if they offer to repair leaks on customers' land without charging?
   d) Why are water meters unfair to families with several children?

2. Make lists of the ways you could save water:
   a) at school   b) at home.

3. Do you think the Environment Correspondent has written a balanced report? Explain your answer.

Now try these

1. Pretend you are the reporter who wrote this article. Your editor has said it is far too long, and you must rewrite it to about half its present length. This means you can use approximately 150 words, but you mustn't leave out any essential information!

2. Prepare a design for a poster that is intended to promote one of the saving tips.

3. Do you think we should be able to use as much water as we want whenever we want, or should we be "more conservation minded"? Give reasons for your answer.

The Phantom Tollbooth

"It seems to me that almost everything is a waste of time," Milo remarks as he walks dejectedly home from school. That is until he mysteriously finds his way into the magical forest of words and numbers.

'Isn't it beautiful?' gasped Milo.

'Oh, I don't know,' answered a strange voice. 'It all depends on how you look at things.'

'I beg your pardon?' said Milo, for he didn't see who had spoken.

'I said it depends how you look at things,' repeated the voice.

Milo turned around and found himself staring at two very neatly polished brown shoes, for standing directly in front of him (if you can use the word 'standing' for someone suspended in mid-air) was another boy just about his age, whose feet were easily three feet off the ground.

'For instance,' continued the boy, 'if you happened to like deserts, you might not think this was beautiful at all.'

'For instance,' said the boy again, 'if Christmas trees were people and people were Christmas trees, we'd all be chopped down, put up in the living room, and covered with tinsel, while the trees opened our presents.'

'What does that have to do with it?' asked Milo.

'Nothing at all,' he answered, 'but it's an interesting possibility, don't you think?'

'How do you manage to stand up there?' for this was the subject that most interested him.

'I was about to ask you a similar question,' answered the boy, 'for you must be much older than you look to be standing on the ground.'

'What do you mean?' Milo asked.

'Well,' said the boy, 'in my family everyone is born in the air, with his head at exactly the height it's going to be when he's an adult, and then we all grow towards the ground. When we're fully grown up, or as you can see, grown down, our feet finally touch. Of course, there are a few of us whose feet never reach the ground, no matter how old we get, but I suppose it's the same in every family.'

He hopped a few steps in the air, skipped back to where he started, and then began again.

'You certainly must be very old to have reached the ground already.'

'Oh no,' said Milo seriously, 'In my family we all start on the ground and grow up, and we never know how far until we actually get there.'

'What a silly system.' The boy laughed. 'Then your head keeps changing its height and you always see things in a different way? Why, when you're fifteen things won't look at all the way they did when you were ten, and at twenty everything will change again.'

'I suppose so.' said Milo, for he had never really thought about the matter.

'We always see things from the same angle,' the boy continued. 'It's much less trouble that way. Besides it makes more sense to grow down and not up.
When you're very young, you can never hurt yourself falling down if you're in mid-air, and you certainly can't get into trouble for scuffing up your shoes or marking the floor if there's nothing to scuff them on and the floor is three feet away.'

Norton Juster

Do you remember?

Copy this paragraph. Fill each gap.

Milo found himself staring at two brown ____1____, about ____2____ feet off the ground! "If people were ____3____ trees, we'd all be chopped down," said the stranger. "In my ____4____," went on the boy, "everyone is born in the ____5____, with his ____6____ the height it's going to be when he's an ____7____. There are a few of us whose ____8____ never reach the ____9____."

More to think about

1. Write a sentence to answer each question.
   a) What did Milo think was beautiful?
   b) Why did the strange boy suggest some people might not find forests beautiful?
   c) What fascinated Milo most about the strange boy?
   d) Why did the boy assume Milo was older than he looked?
   e) What did the boy think would be the main disadvantage of starting on the ground and growing upwards?

2. Do you think Milo has learned something from meeting the strange boy? If so, what do you think he has learned and how might it affect him?

Now try these

1. a) Make a list of the advantages the boy gives for being able to float above the ground.
   b) Make a list of any other advantages you can think of.
   c) What would you most like to do if you could float in the air? Give your reasons.

2. From what you can tell from the passage, describe the characters of Milo and the strange boy. Do you think they are similar people or are they very different?

3. Many stories have been written, and many films made, where people are able to do things that are really impossible except in our fantasies. Write about your favourite 'fantasy' story and say what it is about the story that you particularly like.

Lennie was a television addict. When he was supposed to be doing his homework his eyes would wander towards the TV set. One day, while supposedly doing his homework, he drifted off to sleep.

'And now, Lennie, you have won over three thousand dollars in cash and merchandise and, more important, you have won the chance to spin our Vacation Wheel. How do you feel about that, Lennie?'

'Real good, sir.'

'Then join me over here at the Vacation Wheel. Now, Lennie, I don't have to remind you that up there on the wheel are twenty, all-expenses paid vacations to places all over the world, do I?'

'No, sir.'

'That's twenty, all-expenses paid vacations! You can go to Rome, to London, to Paris. You can go to beautiful Hawaii, exotic Mexico or sunny Spain. All in all, there are twenty, all-expenses paid vacations up there on the wheel. But, Lennie, as you know, there are also what we call zonk trips. How do you feel about those, Lennie?'

'Well, I hope I don't get one.'

'And that's what we're all hoping too, aren't we, folks? Hear that applause, Lennie? They're all with you. Now step up close to the Vacation Wheel. That's right. The three zonk trips as we call them are here and here and here. Try not to land on them.'

'I will, sir.'

'All right, put up your hand now, Lennie, right here on the Vacation Wheel, and Lennie, *give it a spin*!'

'Here goes!'

'Good boy! The wheel is spinning, folks, Lennie really gave it a good spin, didn't he? Where do you want to go Lennie?'

'Any of those places is all right with me.'

'Except the zonk places, right?'

'Right!'

'It's still spinning, and now it's beginning to slow down. Watch the wheel, folks. Where is Lennie going? To Paris? Rome? London? It's almost stopped. It looks like *Egypt*! No! *Rio*! No! *Oh, no!* Look at that! Lennie, you have landed on number thirteen, one of our zonk trips, and I don't have to tell you what that means.'

'It means that I'm going to have to take a zonk trip.'

'Right.'

'Where?'

'Well, let me look in my zonk envelope. Oh, Lennie.'

'What?'

'Oh, Lennie.'

'What? What is it?'

'*Oh, Lennie!*'

'What? I want to know. What is it?'

'Lennie, you are going to have to spend one night, all expenses paid, in a *haunted house*!'

'A what?'

'Yes, Lennie, you heard correctly, you are going to Haunted House Number Thirteen located right on the outskirts – that's the dark, scary outskirts, I might add – of beautiful downtown –'

'But I don't want to spend the night in any haunted house.'

'Of course you don't, but you take your chances, Lennie, just like all the other contestants. Remember that paper you signed when you came on the show?'

'Yes, but I didn't – I mean I couldn't – I mean –'

'Oh, all right, Lennie, I tell you what I'm going to do. You go to the haunted house, spend one night there, and if you survive – I say, if you survive – then come back next week and we'll let you spin the Vacation Wheel again. How about that?'

'But, sir, couldn't I take my three thousand in cash and merchandise and –'

'How many want to see him take the cash and merchandise and go home?'

Silence.

'How many want to see him go to the *haunted house*?'

Wild applause.

'But, sir –'

'See, the audience is with you. Hear that applause? Well, it's time for a commercial break now, but stay with us, folks, for the second half of *Give It a Spin*, the show where *you* pick your prizes and *we* see that you take them…'

Betsy Byars

Do you remember?

Read these sentences about the story. Write 'true', 'false' or 'can't tell' for each one.

1. Lennie's favourite programme was *Give It a Spin*.

2. One day he was invited to be a contestant on *Give It a Spin*.

3. There were twenty all-expenses paid holidays on the Vacation Wheel.

4. There were also twenty zonk trips.

5. The worst zonk trip was to the haunted house.

6. Lennie was pleased to have won his zonk trip.

7. He was told he could have a holiday to anywhere he chose if first he stayed in the haunted house.

8. Lennie asked if he could take the cash rather than the trip.

More to think about

Write a sentence to answer each question.

1. What clues tell us that this is an American story?

2. Do you think that at first Lennie was pleased to be on the show?

3. When and why did his attitude about the show change?

4. What reasons made it difficult for him to turn down his zonk trip?

5. How does the author make this into a rather frightening situation?

6. How does it make you feel about the host of the programme?

7. What do you feel for Lennie by the end of the passage?

Now try these

1. Rewrite the story in your own words, describing what happened, rather than writing it as a conversation.

2. What do you think happened next? Write your own ending for the story.

3. Write about your worst nightmare. Explain why it was particularly frightening.

Hiawatha's Childhood

The Song of Hiawatha is based on American Indian stories and legends. These verses are about Hiawatha's early life.

By the shores of Gitche Gumee,
By the shining Big-Sea-Water,
Stood the wigwam of Nokomis,
Daughter of the Moon, Nokomis.
Dark behind it rose the forest,
Rose the black and gloomy pine-trees,
Rose the first with cones upon them;
Bright before it beat the water,
Beat the clear and sunny water,
Beat the shining Big-Sea-Water.

There the wrinkled, old Nokomis
Nursed the little Hiawatha,
Rocked him in his linden cradle,
Bedded soft in moss and rushes,
Safely bound with reindeer sinews;
Stilted his fretful wail by saying.
'Hush! The Naked Bear will get thee!'
Lulled him into slumber, singing,
'Ewa-yea! My little owlet!
Who is this, that lights the wigwam?
With his great eyes lights the wigwam?
Ewa-yea! My little owlet!'

Many things Nokomis taught him
Of the stars that shine in heaven;
Showed him Ishkoodah, the comet,
Ishkoodah, with fiery tresses;
Showed the Death-Dance of the spirits.
Warriors with their plumes and war-clubs,
Flaring far away to northward
In the frosty nights of Winter;
Showed the broad, white road in heaven,
Pathway of the ghosts, the shadows,
Running straight across the heavens,
Crowded with the ghosts, the shadows.

At the door on Summer evenings
Sat the little Hiawatha;
Heard the whispering of the pine-trees,
Heard the lapping of the water,
Sound of music, words of wonder;
'Minne-wawa!' said the pine-trees,
'Mudway-aushka!' said the water.

Saw the moon rise from the water,
Rippling, rounding from the water,
Saw the flecks and shadows on it,
Whispered, 'What is that, Nokomis?'
And the good Nokomis answered:
'Once a warrior, very angry,
Seized his grandmother, and threw her
Up into the sky at midnight;
Right against the moon he threw her;
'Tis her body that you see there.'

Then the little Hiawatha
Learned of every bird its language,
Learned their names and all their secrets,
How they built their nests in Summer,
Where they hid them in the Winter,
Talked with them whene'er he met them,
Called them 'Hiawatha's Chickens'.
Of all the beasts he learned the language,
Learned their names and all their secrets,
How the beavers built their lodges,
Where the squirrels hid their acorns,
How the reindeer ran so swiftly,
Why the rabbit was so timid,
Talked with them whene'er he met them,
Called them 'Hiawatha's Brothers'.

H.W. Longfellow

55

Do you remember?

Copy these sentences. Fill each gap.

1. The wigwam stood by the shores of _____ _____.
2. It was the wigwam belonging to _____, Daughter of the _____.
3. Behind it was a large _____, with many _____ trees.
4. It was here that Nokomis nursed _____.
5. She called him her little _____.
6. She showed him many things, including _____, the comet.
7. Nokomis also told him the story of the _____ who threw his _____ at the moon.
8. Hiawatha called the birds his _____ and the animals his _____.

More to think about

1. Write a sentence to answer each question.
   a) Do we know whether Nokomis was Hiawatha's mother?
   b) Who else could she have been?
   c) How was Hiawatha's cradle constructed?
   d) Explain what the poet meant by "Saw the moon rise from the water".
   e) Why was it important for Hiawatha to learn about the natural world?

2. Nokomis taught Hiawatha about the sky at night, the stars, the constellations, the Milky Way and many other things.
   a) What was Ishkoodah?
   b) What were its "fiery tresses"?
   c) What was "the Death-Dance of the spirits. Warriors with their plumes and war-clubs"?
   d) What was "the broad, white road in heaven, Pathway of the ghosts"?

Now try these

1. Using your own words, write a detailed description of how you imagine the countryside and surroundings where Hiawatha grew up.

2. As you read this poem to yourself you will notice that it has a strong rhythm. What does it remind you of?

3. Using the poem and other information you might find on the internet or in reference books, make lists of the best and worst things about being an American Indian child in North America 150 years ago.

Martin's Mice

Martin is no ordinary kitten. To everybody's embarrassment, he prefers tinned cat food to real mice.

Pretty little things! He mused. They shall not suffer because of me. I shall never catch one. But though his intentions were good, his instincts, handed down to him through generations of expert mousers, were too strong, and he caught the very first mouse he met.

At the time, he was exploring, in a loft over an old cart-shed. In the days that followed after his mother had left the kittens to their own devices, Martin had done a lot of exploring. Unlike the others, who were always busy hunting, he had plenty of time to wander round the farm. Already he had learned a number of lessons that a farm kitten needs to know.

Cows have big feet that can easily squash you; sows get angry if you go too near their piglets; broody hens are bad tempered birds; and collie-dogs chase cats.

Humans, Martin was glad to find, didn't chase cats. The farmer paid little attention to him, but the farmer's wife made sure he had enough to eat, and the farmer's daughter actually made quite a fuss of him, picking him up and cuddling him.

One day she took Martin to see her rabbits; three white rabbits with pink eyes, that she kept in three large hutches at the bottom of the garden. Why did she keep them, he wondered?

The next time that Martin met his mother on his journeys, he asked her about this.

"Mother," he said, "Why does that girl keep those rabbits?"

"As pets," Dulcie Maude said.

"What's a pet?"

"A pet is an animal that humans keep because they like it. They like looking after it, feeding it, stroking it, making a fuss of it."

"So we're pets, are we?"

"Strictly speaking, I suppose. Dogs certainly are, always fussing around humans, sucking up to them."

'What about cows, and pigs, and sheep?"

"No, they're not pets," said Dulcie Maude. "Humans eat them, you see."

"But they don't eat cats and dogs?"

"Of course not."

"And they don't eat rabbits?"

"Yes, they eat rabbits, but not pet rabbits."

"Why not?"

As with most mothers, there was a limit to Dulcie Maude's patience.

"Oh, stop your endless questions, Martin, do!" she snapped. "Curiosity, in case you don't know, killed the cat!" and she stalked off, swishing her tail.

It was curiosity, nevertheless, that led Martin to climb up the steep steps into the cart-shed loft to see what was in it. What was in it, in fact, was a load of junk. The farmer never threw anything away, in case it should come in useful some day, and the loft was filled with boxes of this and bags of that, with broken tools and disused harness and worn-out coats and empty tins and bottles that once contained sheep-dip or cow-drench or horse-liniment.

Against one wall stood an old white-enamelled bath with big brass taps and clawed caste-iron feet, and it was while Martin was exploring beneath it that something suddenly shot out.

Automatically he put his paw on it.

"I'm most awfully sorry!" he said, but the fat mouse only continued to say "Mercy! Mercy!" in a quavering voice. It seemed to be rooted to the spot, and it stared up at Martin with its round black eyes as though hypnotised.

How pretty it looks, thought Martin. What a dear little thing!

"Don't be frightened," he said.

"It's not for myself alone that I beg you to spare me," said the mouse. "You see, I am pregnant."

What a strange name, thought Martin. I've never heard of anyone called that before.

"How do you do?" he said. "I'm Martin."

What a dear little thing, he thought again. I'd like to look after it, to feed it, to stroke it, to make a fuss of it, just as Mother said that humans like to do with their pets.

After all, he thought, some humans eat rabbits but some keep them as pets. So, in the same way, some cats eat mice, but some…

"Shall I tell you what I'm going to do with you?" he said.

"I know what you're going to do," said the mouse wearily. "After you've finished tormenting me, you're going to eat me."

"You're wrong," said Martin.

He bent his head and gently picked up the mouse in his mouth. Then he looked about him. Then he climbed onto an old wooden chest that stood handily beside the bath, and looked down into its depths.

The perfect place, he thought excitedly. My little mouse can't escape – the plug's still in the plug-hole and the sides are much too steep and slippery – but I can jump in and out easily. He jumped in and laid his burden gently down.

The mouse lay motionless. Its eyes were shut, its ears drooped, its coat was wet from the kitten's mouth.

"Shall I tell you what I'm going to do?" said Martin again.

"Kill me," said the mouse feebly. "Kill me and have done."

"Not on your life!" said Martin. "I'm going to keep you for a pet!"

Dick King-Smith

Do you remember?

Write a sentence to answer each question.

1. Why was Martin no ordinary kitten?
2. What happened when he saw his first mouse?
3. Where did he catch his first mouse?
4. What did Martin learn about collie-dogs?
5. Which of the humans made the biggest fuss of Martin?

More to think about

1. Write three sentences about:
   a) where Martin lived.
   b) the humans who lived on the farm.
   c) Martin's mother.

2. Write a sentence to answer each question.
   a) Why did Martin get confused about whether rabbits were pets or not?
   b) How do you think the saying 'curiosity killed the cat' first came about?
   c) What is meant when the author says the mouse was "rooted to the spot"?
   d) What did he think was the mouse's name? Why was this?

Now try these

1. Pretend you are judging a story writing competition. Score this passage from *Martin's Mice* by Dick King-Smith out of 10. Give the reasons for your decision, saying why you either liked or didn't like the extract. Write about:
   a) how well he develops the characters.
   b) how clearly he describes the setting.
   c) how cleverly the plot unfolds.
   d) how much you are amused by the way he describes the situations.

2. What do you think might happen next in the story? Write your plan for the next chapter.

3. Imagine you are the mouse in the passage. Write about your feelings from the moment that Martin trapped you under his paw.

Unit 20

Deserts

Where are deserts located?

Few people in the world live in inhospitable deserts. Most of us live where the weather is wetter and less harsh. But almost every continent has deserts, either hot deserts or cold deserts.

The map shows where the main hot deserts are located. Notice first that there are no hot deserts in the far north or far south of the Earth. Nor are there any on the Equator. The Equator is an imaginary line around the centre of the Earth, separating the Northern Hemisphere from the Southern Hemisphere. Most of the major deserts lie in the two bands north and south of the Equator, along lines of latitude called the Tropic of Cancer and the Tropic of Capricorn.

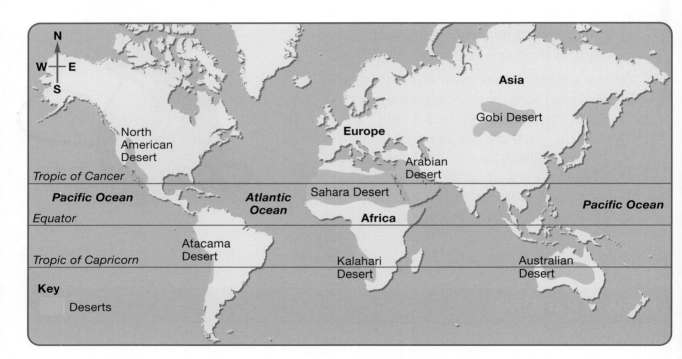

How are hot deserts formed?

The formation of hot deserts involves a lack of precipitation.

Clouds form when water vapour in the air cools and forms tiny drops of water. When the drops become too heavy to stay in the air, the water falls to the ground as rain.

Usually there is water vapour in the air, but sometimes the winds bring very dry air. These winds have already lost their water vapour because they have dropped it as rain over hills and mountains, as is shown in the diagram of the west coast of the United States.

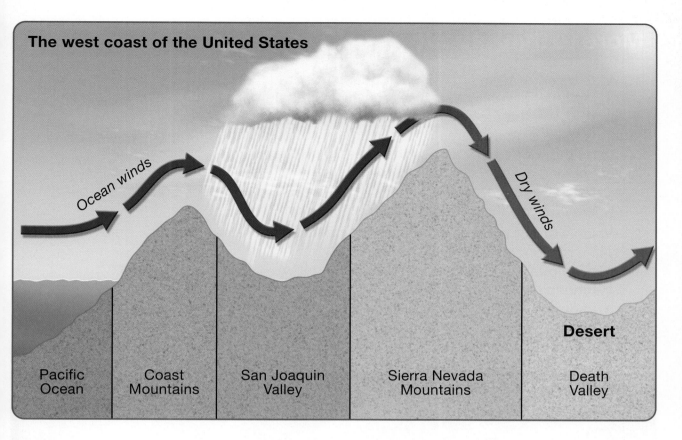

The west coast of the United States

Ocean winds

Dry winds

Desert

| Pacific Ocean | Coast Mountains | San Joaquin Valley | Sierra Nevada Mountains | Death Valley |

Other winds are dry because they are far from an ocean, or because they are very cold. Cold winds blowing across cold ocean currents can't collect much water vapour.

As these dry winds pass across land, no rain falls because there is no water vapour held in the air. Therefore the land remains dry and deserts are formed.

Do you remember?

1. Find the answer to each of these questions by looking at the map.
   a) Which is the biggest desert in Africa?
   b) Name the deserts through which the Tropic of Capricorn passes.
   c) What is the name of the desert in the centre of Asia?
   d) Are there any major deserts in Europe?
   e) Which large island, crossed by one of the tropics, is more than half desert?

2. Find the answers to each of these questions by looking at the diagram.
   a) Over which ocean do the winds blow?
   b) Name the first range of mountains the winds cross.
   c) What happens in the San Joaquin Valley?
   d) What is the second range of mountains called?
   e) When the winds have crossed these mountains, are they wet or dry?

More to think about

1. Write a sentence to answer each question.
   a) Most people enjoy sunshine, so why do very few live in the deserts of the world?
   b) Why aren't there any major deserts in Europe?
   c) Is there a greater area of desert to the north or south of the Equator?
   d) As the winds blow across the oceans, do they gain or lose moisture?
   e) Looking at the diagram, describe why the winds are dry by the time they reach Death Valley.
   f) Why do you think Death Valley has that name?

2. Which word or phrase in each list means the same as each word in bold?
   Use a dictionary to help you.
   a) **precipitation**   waterfall   rain and snow   clouds   wind
   b) **inhospitable**   a hospital   unfriendly   unwell   unusual
   c) **vapour**   moisture in the air   medicine   wind   rainfall
   d) **ocean**   river   large sea   current   large ship

Now try these

1. Use a reference book or an encyclopaedia and make notes about one of the deserts shown on the map.

2. Use your notes and the information in this unit to prepare a presentation about one of the deserts shown on the map.

3. Deserts are inhospitable places to live, and survival can be almost impossible. Imagine that you are one of three passengers in a small aircraft that crashes in a desert; the pilot and all three passengers survive. Describe your struggle to reach an oasis in the distance.

Why Bats Fly at Night

The bat and the bush-rat were always seen in each other's company. Together they went hunting, finding good things to eat, and each evening they would take turns to cook the meal, and then they would eat it together. But in spite of this, the bat did not like the bush-rat, in fact he hated him!

One evening the bush-rat asked, 'Why is your soup always so much better than mine, Bat? Will you show me how to make it?'

'Certainly,' said the bat, a devious plan already forming in his mind.

So the following day the bat prepared the soup as usual, and again it was truly an excellent soup. Then he hid the pot and found another, identical, which he filled with warm water. Soon, as expected, Bush-Rat appeared with his usual cheerful demeanour. 'Hello, Bat, you are going to teach me how to make your delicious soup, aren't you?'

'Most certainly, just watch me,' said the wicked bat. 'You see,' he went on, 'I always boil *myself* in the soup just before the soup is served, and because my flesh is so sweet, it gives the soup its very special flavour.'

Bush-Rat was stunned, and watched with amazement as the bat brought out the pot that contained warm water, into which he jumped. 'You see, this is the boiling soup, and it will taste just perfect!'

The next day was Bush-Rat's turn to provide supper. As usual, the meal was coming together nicely, and so with the soup almost ready he sent his wife away from the fire, telling her that no one must know the bat's secret recipe.

Into the boiling caldron leapt the naïve bush-rat: a fatal mistake!

On returning to the kitchen Bush-Rat's poor wife became totally distraught. She went wailing to the village chief, telling him what Bat had done. The chief immediately issued instructions for the bat to be arrested.

By chance the bat had been flying over the chief's house and heard the order for his arrest being given, so he fled to a nearby cave.

For many days to come, the people hunted for Bat, but he kept quite still high in the cave roof. But eventually he became hungry, very hungry, and that night flew out to find food. And to this day he will only venture out at night to hunt for food, when no one can see or catch him.

Do you remember?

Write the correct answer to each question.

1. How often were Bat and Bush-Rat seen together?
   a) most of the time   b) occasionally   c) never

2. What did they do together each evening?
   a) play games   b) cook and eat   c) just talk

3. What did Bat think of Bush-Rat?
   a) he loved him dearly   b) he was quite friendly   c) he hated him

4. Who found Bush-Rat's dead body?
   a) the chief   b) his wife   c) his children

5. What did the chief do about the crime?
   a) nothing   b) tried to arrest Bat   c) threw Bat into jail

6. Where did Bat hide?
   a) at home   b) in a cave   c) in the forest

More to think about

1. Write a sentence to answer each question.
   a) Why would Bush-Rat not have expected Bat to cause him harm?
   b) Which of the two creatures was the better cook?
   c) Why did Bat need two pots to carry out his deadly plan?
   d) Why did Bush-Rat fall for Bat's deadly scheme?
   e) Why would it have been difficult to have found Bat in the cave?

2. Copy these two lists side by side. Use a dictionary to help you match the words that have similar meanings. The first one has been done to help you.

words from the passage	words or phrases the writer could have used instead
identical	dare to go out
demeanour	deadly
delicious	cunning
devious	outward behaviour
naïve	exactly the same
fatal	gorgeous
distraught	simple and trusting
venture	deeply upset

Now try these

1. Write a summary of the story, including all the essential facts, using no more than six sentences.

2. Folk tales that are apparently about animals, like this one, are really about people and how they behave. Write in your own words what this folk tale can teach us about how people can sometimes act towards one another.